W9-AQR-808

Elephant Baby

the story of Little Tembo

by Ann McGovern
pictures by Fred Brenner

SCHOLASTIC INC. NEW YORK • TORONTO • LONDON • AUCKLAND • SYDNEY

For Charlie

No part of this publication may be reproduced in whole or in part, or stored in a retrieval system, or transmitted in any form or by any means, electronic, mechanical, photocopying, recording, or otherwise, without written permission of the publisher. For information regarding permission, write to Scholastic Inc., 730 Broadway, New York, N.Y. 10003.

ISBN 0-590-31282-0

Text copyright © 1982 by Ann McGovern. Illustrations copyright © 1982 by Fred Brenner. All rights reserved. Published by Scholastic Inc.

12 11 10 9 8 7 6 5 4 0 1 2 3/9

Printed in the U.S.A. 08

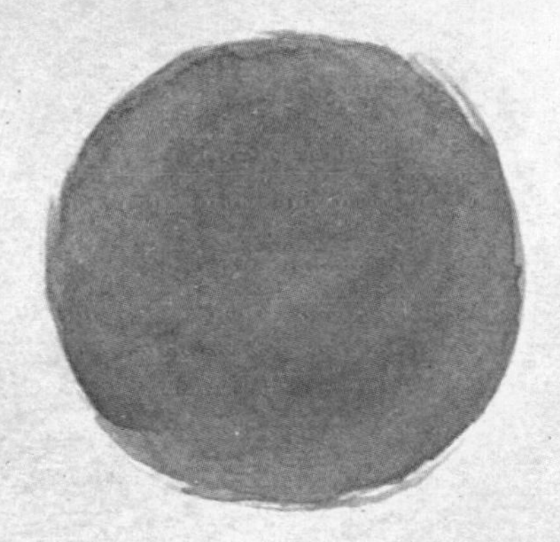

Nine elephants are slowly walking toward the river.
They move silently on thickly padded feet.

Tembo is only two days old.
She is covered with red, wavy hair.
Her little legs wobble as she hurries along
behind her mother.

Suddenly the leader raises her trunk.
She sniffs. She smells danger close by.
Her huge ears spread wide.
She twirls her trunk — a sign that she is nervous.

Nearby, three hyenas are crouching in the bushes.
Hyenas sometimes kill baby elephants!

The big elephant trumpets a loud warning call.
Three other elephant families are not far away.
They hear the leader's trumpeting call,
and follow her sound.

Now there are 40 elephants to fight the danger.
The entire kinship herd has gathered together.

Quickly the big elephants form a circle.
They push and pull the young elephant calves
into the middle.
Tembo is hidden in the circle of big elephants.
The hyenas can't get her.
She is safe — this time.

When Tembo was born, she weighed 250 pounds —
more than a very large man.
Her mother weighs 50 times as much!

Grown female elephants, called *cows*,
are gentle and kind to the young calves.
Tembo's mother does not let her baby
out of her sight.

Tembo's older sister takes special care of her too.
She strokes the baby with her trunk.
She helps her up when she falls.

Tembo is always hungry.
Many times a day she drinks the milk
from her mother's body.

Sometimes Tembo nurses from the leader of the herd, called the *matriarch*
(mate-ree-ark).
Tembo's nine-year-old sister nurses too.
Most elephants nurse until they are about eleven years old.

Tembo lives in the country of Kenya, in Africa.
She travels with her family as they search
for food and water.
They walk through swamps and forests
and along the shores of rivers and lakes.

The three other elephant families that make up
Tembo's large kinship herd are never far behind.
Tembo will get to know her grandmother, cousins,
aunts, sisters, and young brothers.

But she will never know her father.
Grown male elephants, called *bulls*,
do not live with the group.

When a bull is about 12 years old, he is pushed out
of the herd by the female elephants.
He may stay near his family for several years.
Or he may join other lone bulls for a while.
From time to time he will visit an elephant group
to mate with a female.

Tembo is six months old.
She has lost her baby looks.
Her red hair is gone and she is fatter.

Tembo loves the water.
She splashes in the watering hole and squirts other elephants.
Sometimes she takes a mudbath.
Mud and dirt are good for elephants.
When the mud dries, it forms a coat.
Annoying insects can't bite the elephant's skin.

Elephants are good swimmers.
They can swim for more than six hours at a time.
They breathe through their trunks
and can swim with only the tips of their trunks
showing above the water.

One day a bus, carrying tourists, comes racing
along the bumpy road.
The driver is going much too fast.
The bus crashes into the bushes,
very close to where Tembo and her family are feeding.
Tires screech. Tourists scream.
It is too much for Tembo.
She takes off, running as fast as her little legs
can carry her.

Her older sister runs faster.
She runs in front of Tembo to stop her.
She touches Tembo with her trunk as if to say,
"It's all right. You're safe now."
Then she puts the tip of her trunk in Tembo's mouth.
She leads the frightened elephant back to her mother.

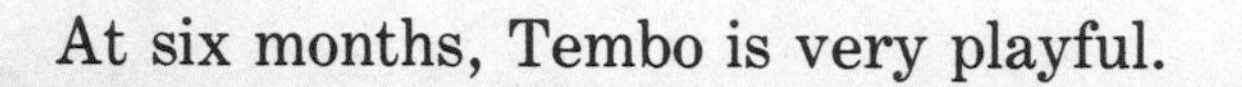

At six months, Tembo is very playful.
She shoves the older elephants.
Sometimes she climbs on top of them when they are lying down.

Elephants rest a few times a day, especially when it's hot.
They even snore!

Sometimes an elephant rests standing up.
It will stand under a shady tree
for as long as five hours.
Only its huge ears move. They flap slowly back and forth
like fans to cool the elephant's body.

Tembo learns something new every week.
She learns how to sit up, sprawl on her tummy,
and roll on her back.
She tries to *charge*.
A charge is an elephant attack.

She tries to make the same charging sound the big elephants make —
a deep, trumpeting call.
But Tembo is still little
and she can only make a high squealing sound.

The hardest thing for Tembo to learn is how to use her trunk.
She doesn't know what to do with the strange, long thing.
Sometimes she trips over it.
Sometimes she just sits on the ground
and puts the tip of it in her mouth.

She will use her trunk in many ways.
She will dig in the sand with it to find water.
She will pluck grass with it.
She will use it for throwing mud and sand and water on her back.
She will greet other elephants with it.
She may even use it to pick up a twig to scratch an itchy leg.
But mostly she will use it for smelling, touching,
tasting, breathing, drinking, and feeding.

Tembo and her family are always looking for food.
They are on the move before the sun is up.
A big elephant eats about 300 pounds of food a day.
It takes an elephant about 16 hours to eat that much.
A big elephant can reach as high as a giraffe
to get leaves from tall trees.

If the tree is too tall, an elephant can send it crashing down.

Monkeys chatter and scurry down from the trees.

Baboons screech.

Antelopes and zebras run to safety.

Every year in Africa, there is a rainy season and a dry season.
In the rainy season,
there is usually plenty to eat for all the animals.
But in the dry season, the grasses and plants dry up and turn brown.
The watering holes dry up too.
The water is only a trickle beneath the sand.

Mother Elephant is scooping out a hole in the sand
to reach the water below.
Tembo wants water too.
She tries to push her mother aside.
Mother Elephant shoves Tembo away.
Tembo has learned another lesson.
She must wait until the big elephants finish drinking.
If she's lucky, there will be a little water left for her.

When Tembo is two, her tusks begin to show.
They will keep growing all her life.
Tembo tries out her new tusks
by scraping them against a rough tree.
Then she pokes one of the older calves.
The calf pokes her back.
Tusks hurt! Tusks can be a dangerous weapon.

One day, Tembo is playing with a bull calf.
But the play soon turns into a pushing contest.
The bull calf is bigger than Tembo.
He uses just the force he needs to win.
He doesn't hurt Tembo.
He has learned how to control his strength.
Tembo must learn that too.
The elephants try out their strength in contests like this.

Tembo sometimes quarrels with other elephants
at the watering hole.
She waves her trunk and spreads her ears wide.
This is called a *threat display*.
A threat display is usually enough to prevent a real fight.
Elephants seldom fight with other elephants.

And other animals seldom attack them on land.
But in the water elephants are not as safe.
Once Mother Elephant got into a fight with a river crocodile.
When she came out of the water,
she had a sore trunk and a torn ear.

Many years pass.
Tembo is eleven years old.
Her mother has had two more calves,
but she still gives Tembo lots of love.

Tembo no longer likes to play rough
with the older calves.
She likes to play with the little calves.
She is learning how to be a mother.
It won't be long before she has a little elephant of her own.

Soon she will mate with a grown bull elephant.
And 22 months later, she will have her first calf.
She may have 12 calves in her lifetime.

Tembo will reach her full size when she is 30.
Elephants live about 65 years.
Tembo may grow up to be the leader of a big herd.
But she and her calves will always stay close
to the family who helped her grow.

Other See-Saw books by Ann McGovern:

Christopher Columbus
Little Wolf
Little Whale
The Pilgrims' First Thanksgiving
Sharks
Stone Soup
Too Much Noise